Heligan

The Complete Works

Heligan

The Complete Works

Secrets Locked in Silence

Tim Smit

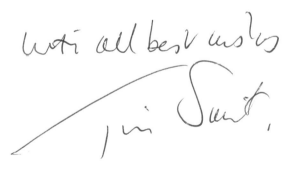

With all best wishes

Tim Smit

4
CHANNEL BOOKS

First published in 1999 by Channel 4 Books, an imprint of Macmillan Publishers Ltd, 25 Eccleston Place, London SW1W 9NF and Basingstoke.

Associated companies throughout the world.

ISBN 0 7522 1734 8

9 8 7 6 5 4 3 2 1

A CIP catalogue record for this book is available from the British Library.

Design by Production Line, Minster Lovell, Oxford
Colour reproduction by Speedscan Ltd
Printed and bound in Italy by New Interlitho, Milan
Photograph credits can be found on page 159.

This book accompanies the Channel 4 television series
made by Cicada/Bamboo Films.
Director: Mike Hutchinson
Producers: Rosemary Forgan and Frances Berrigan

The Lost Gardens of Heligan are at Heligan, Pentewan, St Austell, Cornwall.
Telephone: 01726 845100 Fax: 01726 845101
Website: www.heligan.com e-mail: info@heligan.com

For

ALL THE HELIGAN STAFF

past, present and future.

Dedicated
to the memory of a dear friend,

LIQUERICHE

Daughter of Horace and Doris,
born just before the great storm of 1990;
died as I completed the last words of this book,
November, 1998.

Contents

Introduction

This photograph opens a window on that other world, a golden era peopled only by shadows. For seven years I had lived and breathed Heligan, searching for clues about the people who had once worked here, whose story I wanted to tell. Through sheer determination we had rebuilt their garden structures and through trial and error re-created many of their technologies, the secrets of which had died along with the apprenticeship system. Much like archaeologists studying the Etruscans all we had were artefacts and names, nothing more. These names had become as familiar as old friends yet had remained disembodied. Here, in front of me at last, was a tantalizing glimpse of the past: a unique pictorial record of those working people – a still life where the characters remain for ever frozen in time, the defining cast of the play we wished to reprise.

Taken at the turn of the century by a Mr F. Dalby-Smith (Silver Medallist and Prizeman) of The Studio, Mevagissey, the sepia-tinted photograph is of a formal, posed group of some Heligan staff in front of the great wooden door leading into the Flower Garden. The composition shows seven men standing behind a seated group of three men and a woman. The men are wearing their Sunday best of polished shoes, waistcoats, jackets and ties, their wing collars painfully tight, and they gaze sombrely towards the lens behind which the photographer would have been hidden from view under the black cloth of his plate camera. Like a magician, he was the master of an art which still held the capacity for wonder, not least when his subjects were working people.

All the men are wearing hats, save one who lounges with a slight air of insolence next to the head gardener (and his wife?), resting his hat on his knee. The others are topped with bowlers, cloth caps and a boater, yet this man bears a brushed felt hat with the crown creased down, of the style favoured by government ministers of the time. The older men are bearded whereas the young guns sport moustaches of varying ambition from handlebar to pencil line. The senior men have fob chains attached to the middle buttons of their waistcoats. At the far right-hand side of the picture stands a man a good head taller than the rest, his bowler worn jauntily off-centre, smoking a pipe. However, it is his trousers that catch the eye for they are plus fours, worn with lace-up leggings, puttees and very finely polished shoes. The bailiff, perhaps, used to mixing with the upper classes and affecting their dress code? There at last, as an unprompted loan in the summer of 1997, was a picture, with all its detail in faded glory, of those who ran the estate and gardens in Heligan's finest hours.

But a decade or so after the photograph was taken, some of these very men, seeking the comfort of posterity during the uncertainty of August 1914, may have scrawled their names in pencil on the lime-washed walls of the thunderbox room. Another three-quarters of a century after that, John Nelson and I uncovered these signatures on an early exploration into the almost impenetrable recesses of the smaller of the walled gardens, the productive 'engine room' we would come to know as the Melon Garden.

I was to encounter some of these names yet again on the war memorials at Gorran, Mevagissey and St Ewe. Finding them provided the poignant inspiration for a garden restoration dedicated to telling the story of these people. Not the airbrushed history that fills lifestyle magazines everywhere, but the 'no frills' story of working men and women,

(above left) **Some of the Heligan team, around 1900. Who were they? What happened to them?**

shorn of romantic embellishment; a simple celebration of skills and crafts honed by the needs of a rich, unselfconscious self-sufficiency. Unusually, the passing of these skills was not due to obsolescence, but was the sad consequence of a strange cultural amnesia caused by the trauma of a war that penetrated every fibre of society and changed things for all time. As the new order took over and the future became the touchstone for the nation, the sepia photographs, curling gently at the edges, were stored away. At Heligan the onslaught of nature proved irresistible. Her splendid gardens mutely succumbed to a deep sleep, under a blanket of brambles and mounting piles of fallen timber. Garden structures groaned and crumpled under the weight and horticultural riches were absorbed into the encroaching wilderness, to remain forgotten by all but a few.

Only by chance did we come across our 'Sleeping Beauty', and it was the purest serendipity that led us to draw together a team of people with the passion, commitment and competence to reinstate the fabric of this gently melancholy, yet magical, place. In so doing, unwittingly and over time, we created a staff which grew to mirror that which walked this stage in Heligan's heyday. They are the living proof, were it needed, that we are bringing the gardens back to the breadth of structure and order they previously commanded. This journey of discovery has required a combination of explorer's zeal, detective work, craftsman's skill and a drive and endurance that can only come from a labour of love. And so the main story we set out to tell, of the 'ordinary' men and women who once made this garden great, is starting to unfold.

In all the estates of Britain, behind-the-scenes productive gardens were regarded in purely utilitarian terms and therefore taken for granted, much as the kitchens of any big house would have been. A visitor would have been guided around the Pleasure Grounds to enjoy set-piece romantic structures, spectacular plantings from foreign lands and surprising vistas to draw the eye – all of which were intended to give pleasure and reinforce the impression that the host was a man of taste and power. Heligan was no different. Only in exceptional circumstances would visitors have been encouraged to

(right) **The Sundial Garden in spring. The red-brick wall protects the replanted herbaceous border, while an original rhododendron frames a view of the restored sundial in the middle of a fine new lawn.**
(over) **Heligan's superb collection of rhododendrons, some introduced by Sir Joseph Dalton Hooker 140 years ago, defy gravity and enchant visitors to the Pleasure Grounds to this day.**

venture into the productive gardens – perhaps if the squire escorted his guests to view the successful flowering of an unusual plant in his collection, which might have included a potentially prizewinning pineapple or some newly imported hothouse exotic of which he was particularly proud. Ironically, it is these areas which most captivate Heligan's visitors today – and it is not surprising. For this is where most of the workforce is occupied, just as it was 100 or even 150 years ago. Here one finds again the complete range of traditional crop rotation alongside the more demanding collection of glasshouse fruits. The whole operation remains particularly labour intensive and therefore especially vulnerable to forces outside its control.

If the working gardens were seldom considered worthy of outside interest, the working buildings occupied by the garden staff themselves were almost invisible. Offices, potting sheds, stores and bothies were usually built with a northerly aspect against the sides of the walled gardens – the darkest and least desirable locations possible. This invisibility is emphasized by the near absence of a photographic record of these elements of the productive gardens. It is unlikely that the squire would have contemplated taking pictures of everyday working life. The capture of a horticultural curiosity on film – the giant gunnera leaf held by a gardener in front of the pineapple pit in the Melon

HELIGAN, HYDRANGEA WALK.

Garden or the proud achievement of a fine range of glasshouses in the Flower Garden – is an exceptional rarity. The staff would not have been able to afford cameras, even had they considered their daily lives worth recording.

However, many areas of the Pleasure Grounds, including the Jungle, found a place in the family album, particularly from 1890 onwards, and we were able to use archive photographs to inform our recovery and reconstruction of the Italian Garden, New Zealand, the Ravine, the Rides and the Sundial Garden. The restoration of the key productive areas could only be based on piecing together the remaining bones of the past and on research into the traditional varieties that would have been grown there.

Today, even an innocent visit to Heligan raises a heightened awareness of our forefathers, a driven curiosity about their past which engenders respect for their lifestyle and awe for their achievements. As we count the months until the end of this century there is also the concern that time is running out ... time to glean knowledge from the diminishing bank of living memory that is available to us. Eighty years on from Armistice Day, 11 November 1918, we could join those still alive in saluting the sacrifices made by their families and by their comrades who fell in the Great War. In another decade this will be impossible. In the autumn of 1998, therefore, it seemed appropriate for Heligan to fashion its own commemoration of their loss and, at one remove, ours.

I first met the sculptor Heather Keir-Cross in 1997 when I spoke at a book festival at Dartington College of Arts in Devon, where she was a student. Her enthusiasm for the challenge of working in ice met its match in me and I commissioned six life-size ice creations for an exhibition to be called *Ghosts of Gardeners Past*. Here today, gone tomorrow. Our own garden staff became the physical models for Heather and period details were added later. Months of careful planning and military timing (for ice is an unforgiving medium) produced an exquisite, transitory experience. Dust to dust ... the imagery and allusion proved even more dramatic than planned. And all that now remains of her achievement lies within these pages.

This book offers a photographic record of the remarkable occasion of the Ice Sculpture Exhibition, a tribute to gardeners past (and indeed, ironically, to the

(left) **The Hydrangea Walk, otherwise known as Grey Lady's Walk, drew visitors from the Big House into the Pleasure Grounds.**

teamwork of those today). But it primarily illustrates, sometimes by contrast, many of the challenges earlier staff would have had to face and the nature of their achievements, as seen through the eyes of those who work at Heligan now. Provoking comparisons continually arise between their circumstances and our own, and there remain as many questions as there are answers about Heligan's past. Tantalizing glimpses are obscured by the patina of the passing years. However, we begin with the premise that by their deeds shall you know them.

(above) **The camellia is one of a huge collection of early introductions, many of which remain unnamed.**
(right) **Rich pickings. The early summer harvest from the Vegetable Garden includes a wealth of traditional varieties selected for flavour.**

My partner, John Nelson *(above left)*, masterminded the restoration of the buildings. The head gardener's office was retrieved from dereliction in the winter of 1993/94. Our staff includes a small team of builders, as it certainly would have done in the past. Tiggy Duff *(above right)* worked from dawn to dusk *(above)* until the magic moment when a wisp of woodsmoke emerged from the chimney *(above right)*, announcing in papal fashion that the gardens were back in business. Everywhere there was a sense of renewal *(over)*.

The great plant-hunters never undertook a challenge like this. A massive date palm *(Phoenix canariensis)* was moved to the Jungle *(above left)* after an overnight stop in the Flower Garden which ended up lasting eighteen months. Kenneth had prepared a large hole *(left)*. The garden team with Kenneth Renowden *(above, far left)*, are *(top row)* **Dave Burns, Adrian Burrows, Richard Dee, Lander King, Mike Friend,** *(bottom row)* **Charles Fleming, Mike Rundle, Mike Helliwell and Simon Bayly.**

In common with most jungles, Heligan's was almost impenetrable. The original paths meandered down through a steep valley, occasionally branching off onto the higher ground to take advantage of the vistas. Our visitors were unexpectedly curious and intrepid and the passage of thousands of feet soon revealed the vulnerability of this path network. We decided to create a wooden boardwalk to protect the roots of the precious plant collection *(above)*.

Now, with a modicum of good humour, it is possible for visitors to penetrate the lush vegetation of the subtropical interior, through tunnels of bamboo, to explore a vivid and multi-textured green world of swamps and exotic specimens *(right)*.

When necessary we use late twentieth-century equipment and associated expertise, such as earth-moving machinery *(top)* and chainsaws *(above left and right)*. These augment traditional skills which have been practised here since time immemorial. In the Lost Valley, a bucket of hot ash is used to fire a charcoal-burning kiln *(right)*.

The clearance of self-seeded and fallen trees from the estate created mountains of timber which we couldn't bear to waste. From time to time an old tractor-driven planking machine is set up to process it *(above)*. After racking and drying, our home-grown supplies are stored for future needs. John's cabin for the charcoal burners *(right)* was built of rough-cut timber, straight from the woods, but where's the door?

The foundations of a successful Victorian productive garden lay in the meticulous preparation and enrichment of the soil. A heady menu of blood, bones, fishmeal, compost and manures of all sorts was employed by succeeding generations of head gardeners, who kept their art a closely guarded secret. There was a strong French influence in this high regard for the soil. There on the continent, a market gardener would lease space from the landowner, creating or bringing his own soil with him, and going so far as to remove it on carts at the expiry of his tenure.

After our clearance of the overgrown Vegetable Garden, our team was struck by the quality of the awaiting ground. Informed cultivation over generations had created an invaluable, if hugely labour-intensive, inheritance of deep, rich, dark soil. We would have to make a similar and continuing commitment if we were to reap the benefits. Mike Rundle, Charles Fleming and Simon Lawday collect seaweed from Portmellon Cove near Mevagissey *(above)*.

Our staff continue the age-old traditions of soil enrichment, regularly incorporating well-rotted horse manure, home-made composts and fresh seaweed into the ground *(right)*. Our practices largely mirror those of the nineteenth century, save that we forgo the dubious pleasures of 'human night soil'.

The Sundial Garden *(qbove and right)* **is a fine monument to the skills of the in-house building team, led by John Nelson. It shows off their virtuosity in levelling and setting out, bricklaying, cobbling and, with a little help, stonemasonry. With expert advice the herbaceous border was restocked using pre-1880 varieties. Lander King took on a traditional responsibility for the lawns. He considered the scythe, donkey-drawn mowers and steam driven contraptions of the past but rather surprisingly decided to use the lightweight, precision-tooled machinery of today** *(below)*.

1998 was a bumper year for pests. The rabbits went forth and multiplied, eating everything in sight with a brazen disregard for visitors and staff alike. They extended their culinary ambitions beyond the acres of productive garden to the choicest morsels in the Pleasure Grounds, especially the Sundial Garden *(left)* and the Italian Garden *(above)*.

This magnificent pink *Magnolia campbellii* *(above)* holds court over the Dovecote Lawn behind Flora's Green. In addition to her garden responsibilities, Mary Crowle *(above right)* tends the fantail pigeons which her father donated to Heligan from his lofts.

Bees fulfilled a fundamentally important function in eighteenth- and nineteenth-century productive gardens. Honey and wax were highly valued in the local economy, but it was the role of the bee as pollinator that was considered crucial by the head gardener. The presence of the bee bole wall *(over)*, adjacent to the walled gardens, is a demonstration of this. We have returned traditional skeps to a few of the boles within the wall, but do not harvest the honey from these colonies.

Tony Montague, our joiner, has established a new apiary in the Orchard above Lost Valley *(left)*, where the bees feast on the flowers of sycamore and bramble. In the autumn he extracts the highly sought-after **Heligan honey** *(below left and right)*.

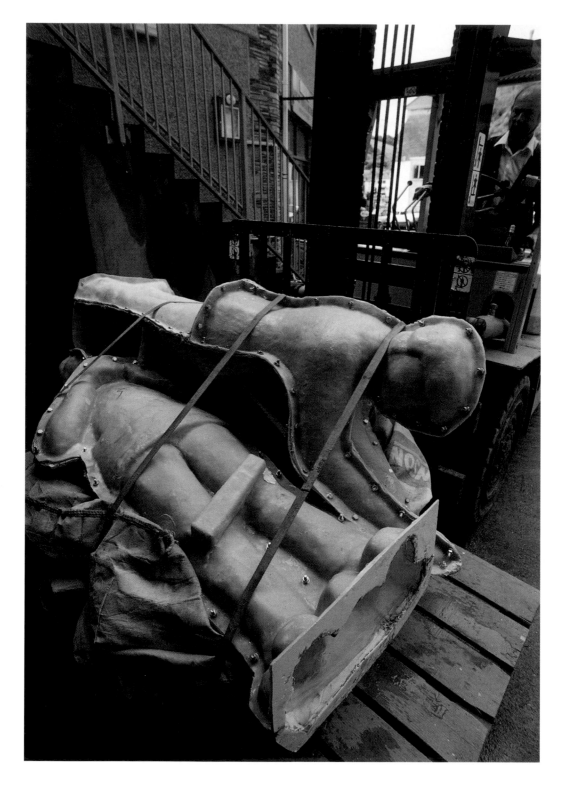

Like strange sarcophagi from an unknown civilization, the life-sized moulds of the ice sculptures lie in state in the Mevagissey cold store. In the autumn of 1998, having emerged from their three-day interment in the freezer, they were then ready to begin their tortuous journey *(left and below)* to their final resting places in the garden.

The Northern Summerhouse is the oldest building in the Pleasure Grounds and was one of the first that we restored. The location of this lovely arch-fronted, small east-facing pavilion was chosen to enable the Squire and his guests to enjoy the superb views across St Austell Bay and beyond, through windows cut or trained into the boundary hedge of the garden.

In 1998 the building team developed the small garden surrounding the Summerhouse, laying an enormous slated paving around a new rectangular lily pool. The first windows were reinstated in our new *Griselinia* hedge, providing a view both into the garden *(above)* and out from the garden *(far right)*. This setting was selected by Heather Keir-Cross for the first of her ice sculptures, The Dreamer, seen here emerging from its mould *(right)*.

The Flower Garden

The Flower Garden lays a special claim on my affections for it was here, inside the ruins of the lean-to vinery, that I first fell under the spell of Heligan and embarked on an adventure that was to determine the course of my life, and which continues to keep a hold on my imagination up to the present day.

In February 1990, accompanied by John Willis who had recently inherited these derelict gardens at the heart of the Tremayne estate, I first broke through into the Flower Garden. The romantic appeal of the overgrown greenhouses was immediate. The warm red-brick walls which enclosed the garden described a territory that felt complete in itself. However, it was a little thing, a small pair of rusty grape scissors hanging from a nail in the vinery wall that really excited my curiosity. I wondered who had worked here, where they had lived, how they had led their lives and what had happened to cause this marvellous place to come to an end with a whimper.

It was the sheer ordinariness of this tenuous yet intimate connection that fired my ambition to make Heligan come alive again.

It is, of course, a romantic deception to imagine that one can genuinely see the world through the eyes of people who were locked within social and economic relationships that no longer exist today. One can, however, come to understand and admire both the ordered sophistication and the sheer hard graft of their husbandry and working practices. Essentially, these met the needs of all who lived and worked here, both owners and staff.

A number of plans found at the County Record Office gave us a good idea of how Heligan's gardens had developed, structurally. In the 1730s a pair of small brick-walled gardens had been built. These we have come to know as the Poultry Yard (which is likely to have housed a mushroom house) and the Nursery Garden. In 1780 the Flower Garden was built using the western walls of these smaller gardens as its own eastern wall. Its restoration began in the autumn of 1993 and culminated in the first harvest of 1995. The major problem facing us was the absence of any photographic record that could inform the framework for our planting plan.

The 1839 tithe map and later the 1880 Ordnance Survey map date and place the greenhouses in the positions we find them today. Scanty written documentation gave us few clues as to their exact functions. Their original construction would have taken place when fashion dictated and as and when the Squires Tremayne and their head gardeners saw fit. Their restoration took place under very different circumstances. We were funded by a mixture of public-sector grants and sponsorship which put us under extreme time pressure. As opposed to the leisurely construction programme that would have prevailed during their original incarnation, we had to rebuild and restore to function all the key greenhouses within a twelve-month period in order to stay within the grant-eligibility criteria.

(above left) **This precious early photograph of the Flower Garden, looking east, is taken from Damaris Tremayne's recently rediscovered album.**

(over) **From the first days of the restoration, teams from the British Trust for Conservation Volunteers, up to twelve strong and from all walks of life, have visited for up to a fortnight at a time. This was one of Jean Griffiths' and George Crumpler's earliest working holidays at Heligan, clearing brambles from the ruins of the orchid house in the Flower Garden, looking west with the vinery behind.**

We were, however, able to take short cuts that had not been available to the original craftsmen. We constructed a large weatherproof polytunnel in the middle of the site which allowed us to work no matter what the conditions. Our craftsmen had the benefit of computer modelling which enabled our suppliers to scan the original timbers in order to replicate them, whereas the early craftsmen had to match timbers by eye. We also had the benefit of electricity, and so we could use power tools to shorten our cutting and assembly times significantly. The large beams for the earliest greenhouse would have been cut in the sawpit next to the Steward's House. The greenhouses erected after 1870 would have had the benefit of the new engine-driven saw, set up inside Shepherd's Barn, one of a number of farm buildings behind Heligan House. All the original greenhouses were built of fine old pitch pine and then painted with lead paint, which is porous and therefore enables the timber to breathe. This system is no longer available to us: pitch pine is hard to find and the use of lead paint is now illegal for health and safety reasons. Today we are therefore forced to use newer pine unless reclaimed timber is available from other sources. New timber can be dipped to make it weatherproof, but then it should not be painted. Modern paint and opaque stains cannot compete in quality with what was previously available.

Health and safety at work was not a national issue at the turn of the century. Different concepts of responsibility prevailed and an accident would be compensated for by the benevolent paternalism of the landowner or his agent. The modern world is a very much more dangerous place with its heavy dependence on machinery. The weight of the law is now, quite rightly, behind the protection of the individual, leaving an employer with the constant threat of litigation. Heligan today suffers from a paradox. Traditional practices are monitored by inappropriate twentieth-century regulations and this sometimes leads to hilarious, but more often debilitating and costly, confusion.

The differences are nowhere more striking than in the use of sprays. In the nineteenth century gardeners applied chemicals to almost everything they grew, both in the open field and in the tight confines of the greenhouse. The obligation to produce perfect specimens for the table led to the widespread application of those infamous pesticides strychnine, nicotina, sulphur and cyanide, by means of brass sprays which were euphemistically christened 'widow-makers' in the gallows humour of their users. Tobacco leaves were soaked in water to make a poisonous brew which was used as a spray, and were also burned in the glasshouses to obtain the same effect: they killed just about everything. Ironically, out of preference, the staff at Heligan today practise a near-organic regime. We use biological methods and organic pest-control measures and employ chemicals only rarely, against intransigent problems (such as knotweed). Strict regulations govern the storage of chemicals and the training and equipment necessary for their use. The spectacular disregard for the dangers of noxious substances in the previous century quite literally takes the breath away.

The twelve-month deadline for constructing the greenhouses was met with little time to spare. We restored the citrus house, vineries, peach house and banana house on the evidence of the existing remains and verified their former use by referring to Victorian garden manuals. We have not yet undertaken the restoration of any of the original heating systems associated with these particular buildings. Their old coal-fired boilers are magnificent and we are hoping that in due course we will be able to get them working again. We are viewing our final structural restoration in the Flower Garden, that of the old stove house (for exotics), as the opportunity to confront this technical challenge. The lengths of cast-iron pipework and the rusting boilers lurking in dank underground hideaways will taunt us until they get steam up once more.

The reinstatement of the central north–south path, the dipping pool at the centre of the Flower Garden and the drains completed a structural restoration that was demanding if fairly straightforward. However, the next stage proved more complex. Our only clue to the Victorian planting plan of the garden (and most surely this would, like everything else, have evolved over the generations), came from an aerial photograph taken in about 1950. This shows a distinctive trapezium shape to the north of Heligan House where the land, by that time, had largely fallen from productive use and the greenhouses were in a state of neglect. Marks in the grass describe a pattern that seems to lack logic for what was, after all, the most sheltered and therefore most valuable of all the productive areas. In truth, when they were marked onto a plan we ascribed them to the route taken by a lawnmower in the course of basic maintenance for the then tenants of the house. We had been told by Fred Draycott, whose father had been head gardener in the 1920s, that when Heligan House was used as a hospital for convalescent officers during the First World

War the eastern half of the Flower Garden (the productive area closest to the house) was adapted to general crop production to service the more basic requirements of the inmates. One further poor snapshot of indeterminate date (but with the orchid house – a late nineteenth-century freestanding replacement to the stove house – still intact) shows an expanse of the garden already gone to seed.

It wasn't until 1998, when John Willis's great-aunt, Damaris Tremayne, presented us with an old family photograph album containing two precious views of the Flower Garden, that we realized to our horror that we had ignored the evidence of our own eyes. In the meantime Philip McMillan Browse, our horticultural adviser from the start, had created a logical and appealing layout based on the geography of the garden and his knowledge of the productive needs of the Big House, guided by the designs of similar gardens of the same period elsewhere. Ironically, as a result our new Flower Garden is possibly set to become even more intensively efficient than the original one, although the vagaries of the British climate have not yet permitted us to establish firm guidelines for successional plantings and harvesting.

Philip was very clear as to the production requirements that would have been expected from the Flower Garden when it was in its prime. A year-round supply of fresh flowers was required, herbs (both aromatic and medicinal), tender vegetables and saladings in season, wall fruits (apricots and cherries), exotic plant specimens from the hothouses and glasshouse fruits including grapes for the table, citrus, figs and peaches. He undertook extensive research to track down the traditional varieties that he wanted to grow again.

Considered in this day and age the demand for cut flowers may seem a little exaggerated. However, a series of photographs from Damaris Tremayne's album tells the story. In the public rooms of Heligan House every surface seems to carry a vase of flowers and at strategic points in the room an exotic pot plant or two catches the eye. An interesting find in the Devon County Record Office in Barnstaple provides a fascinating glimpse into Heligan's world of flowers, dictated by the requirements of the Squires Tremayne throughout most of the last century.

An inventory dated 1909 includes the contents of the Flower Room. John Usmar, a friend and local historian, summarizes:

The reception rooms consisted of Drawing Room, Red Room, Hall with Staircase and Landing, Dining Room, Library, and Smoking Room. In the Drawing Room was a glass flower vase, a three compartment carved marble stand for flower pots and a round oak fluted plant stand. In the Hall was a brass flower pot on an Indian carved rosewood stand, and something called a 'pedestal plush bell metal flower pot on lion's claws'. There were three blue and white vases in the Red Room, and on the Landing was a pair of 'Crested Vases on square stands', and two 'embossed pipes for Pampas Grass'.

The Flower Room held no less than 76 flower vases (mostly glass), ranging in type from 'plain frilled-top', through 'Bottle-shaped', 'Spiral', 'Plain Glass', 'Glazed Brown', 'Square-cut plain', 'Glazed banded', to 'Hat-Top Purple', and 'Fishbowl'. The tallest was 16" but the average was 8". The shortest were the 17 'Square-cut Plain vases' which were only 2¼" to 3½" tall, possibly used by each place at the dinner table.

(left) **Fresh flowers adorn every available surface in the library of Heligan House c. 1895.**
(over) **It is possible, with successional plantings, to enjoy cosmos throughout the entire summer. It grows to hedge height and has unusual feathery foliage.**

Also in the Flower Room was some shelving, a 10ft by 3ft table, a large glazed flower pot, two square parrot cages and a long-spout watercan. The watercan and its user must have been kept busy, for taps were few and far between; but they were in pairs – well water for drinking and reservoir water for everything else. With 6 reception rooms and some of the 21 bedrooms, and 76 vases to decorate them with, cut flowers in quantity were indeed needed.

John Usmar adds a nice little postscript: 'In the inventory the parrot cages were empty, but when there was a parrot in residence it had a place of honour, for in the Drawing Room was a "Mahogany Table for a Parrot".'

During winter, flowers would have been brought to the Big House from other areas as well the Flower Garden. For instance, the dark house in the Melon Garden would have been used to force early scented buds from the bulbs of narcissus, hyacinth and lily of the valley. Precious pots of violets would also have been encouraged inside the cold frames there. Outdoors, the Pleasure Grounds would have yielded superb sprays from the rare collections of rhododendrons and camellias which flowered in glorious succession from late November to the beginning of June. In addition to their requirements for the Big House, the Tremaynes, as the leading local family, would have been responsible for supplying flowers and foliage to decorate surrounding halls and churches, and their subtropical plantings would have produced striking greenery throughout the year.

On their gently, southerly sloping ground, the sheltered beds of the Flower Garden could secure the earliest possible outdoor harvest of salads, with seedlings raised annually in the cold frames of the Melon Garden and then planted out under cloches. Block plantings of the biennial wallflower followed by sweet william would have provided additional form and colour beside the spring-flowering narcissi, ixia, iris and camassia. Early flowering herbaceous plants, ideal for displays, were also grown in small, hedge-lined plots – doronicum, peony and dianthus. Summer bulbs included gladioli, the amazingly named chincerinchee and a host of lilies. And by late June the annually sown varieties of cut flower, set out in long rows for efficiency rather than aesthetics, commenced a succession of flowerings, extending the season well into autumn when the traditional pompom chrysanthemums might stretch a healthy show right through until the end of November. And, of course, a harvest of flowers for drying would have been hung up in readiness to cheer those drab weeks up to Christmas.

There we were, with this colourful, joyous piece of history brought back for the living on a scented breeze. But Philip McMillan Browse and Richard Dee, our present head gardener, had an additional consideration that would not have concerned their nineteenth-century counterparts who were simply generating supplies for the Big House. The Flower Garden then was not a regular destination for family or visitors and therefore did not need to offer on-the-ground – let alone year-round – interest, as it does now. In summer, of course, the garden speaks for itself securing delighted gasps of wonder. In winter our solution is to make a virtue of the freshly prepared bare ground, dressed with seaweed and framed by neatly clipped box hedges. Why not allow visitors to enjoy the mathematical purity required of professional productive horticulture – a purity which provides a stark contrast with the wildness of the Pleasure Grounds and re-emphasizes the point that horticulture is the art of bending nature to the needs of man? Practising the art requires continuous mental effort and physical involvement and offers endless trials and torments in battles against the climate, pests and disease. Yet it is upon this timeless activity that our whole sophisticated society still depends. Some people are as struck by the sight of a lone man digging large tracts of ground as they are by barrows of produce emerging from a prolific harvest. For many of them, these are no longer first-hand experiences.

In the vineries, under Richard Dee's watchful eye, Paul Haywood, our fruit man, has been bringing on a marvellous selection of grapes, chosen for flavour as well as for keeping. Now, once again, we are able to provide this fresh fruit for the Christmas table as used to be the fashion. The excitement of seeing those perfect, bountiful bunches with their delicate bloom hanging in ranks from ceiling to floor is truly splendid. One whimsically wishes that the original owner of those grape scissors could appear and give us his view on the current state of affairs.

For the back walls inside the vineries Philip and Richard have selected a number of exotics, ranging from monstrous sabre-toothed agaves to elegant daturas, which could have been used to grace the public rooms of the Big House. Next to them, in the citrus house, a fine selection of edible, ornamental fruits, which can be wheeled out for

(above) **Old varieties of peach are trained as cordons on wires under the glass of the unheated south-facing peach house. Paul Haywood, our fruit man, has had to take pains to learn the art in the absence of an apprenticeship system, gleaning the necessary skills from the few remaining practitioners able and willing to pass the information on.**

public display as in the past, has been established. Grapefruit, satsumas, Seville oranges, lemons and limes fill the glasshouse. Although they are impressive when they fruit in temperate climes their capacity to delight is diminished by familiarity in the modern age. For this reason Richard is bringing on some other exotic non-citrus varieties, such as papaya and babaco, to see whether we can still generate that original spirit of curiosity.

On the western wall of the garden the peach house is in full production although it has not been without its problems. Bolting rootstock and inexperience with pruning led to the loss of a number of specimens and Paul, determined not to be beaten, was encouraged to go in search of some specific training. This is no longer readily available from the horticultural colleges, and so he tracked down Harry Baker, 'Mr Fruit', the doyen of fruit growers and a man of infinite charm and patience, who took him under his kindly wing. Paul is now able to develop his knowledge and practical skills under Harry's watchful eye, just as he might have done as an apprentice gardener in times gone by.

Appropriate training is a real problem today because most of what is provided by the institutions is dedicated to giving young people a grounding in amenity horticulture. The demise of the great productive gardens like Heligan coincided with the decline and eventual disappearance of apprenticeship, which was based on practice and experience. This is something that the modern education system has never satisfactorily replaced, to the detriment of many traditional skills-based industries. In an era that is becoming increasingly interested in the past it is ironic that the expertise needed to maintain and develop this horticultural heritage is fast disappearing. At Heligan we are determined to make the very best provision for our staff so that we can develop our own self-contained apprenticeship system and in so doing protect the gardens into the future. The existence today of horticultural training colleges is evidence, if any were needed, of how far we have moved from learning within a working environment where practical knowledge was passed down in the context of standards set by a demanding owner.

The quality of the hospitality at the Big House played a significant role in developing the reputation of the family who lived there. Satisfying the demands of a constant stream of house guests and visitors was the task of the cook and butler who, in turn, established their requirements with the head gardener. With the Big House now divorced from its splendid gardens, the squire, his family and friends no longer determine the range of produce grown at Heligan. Yet the gardens must still be managed with an end user in mind: the measure of their success remains the satisfaction they give.

Our head gardener now operates within the context of thousands of visitors. His domain must offer interest and please the eye throughout the year, while supplying a range of fresh produce for their refreshment and flowers for their tables. It sounds easy if you say it quickly enough.

Craftsmen put the finishing touches to the restored citrus house *(left)*. Its gleaming timbers and the shadows of the 'beaver tail' glass on the rear wall serve to emphasize the geometric purity which so satisfied the Victorians. It is hard to believe that this picture is taken from almost the exact spot where I first entered the glasshouses and made my fateful decision to restore the gardens.

As if to say 'this is what it's all about', Philip McMillan Browse *(above)* leans happily against one of the plant-laden shelves on the back wall of the vinery, its function restored. Note the fine cast-iron detail of the shelf brackets and the floor gratings, salvaged from a derelict glasshouse elsewhere which was demolished for development.

Cornwall has little tradition of brickwork, hence supplies of reclaimed bricks are extremely scarce. We eventually found some new bricks to match those of the surrounding eighteenth-century walls. John Nelson undertook the setting out and most of the construction of the herringbone terrace in front of the citrus house and vinery *(above left)*.

With the brick paths complete and the new box hedging planted, the restored Flower Garden welcomed its first spring *(above right)*. The lid of a Victorian cloche is set at an angle as a fine crop of early lettuce gets a breath of fresh air. Behind, wallflowers are ready to pick for the table.

With regimental precision Mike Friend *(below)* continues a tradition hundreds of years old, painstakingly sowing seeds in straight lines along a string. The eastern, south-facing half of the Flower Garden is the most sheltered and valuable growing area at Heligan. Tender vegetables, saladings and herbs are raised in small box-edged plots *(over)*, interspersed with crops of perennial or annual colour such as marigolds *(right)*. In 1998 Mike came by the rare seed of the Tall Scotch Prize marigold dating back to 1824.

The western half of the Flower Garden is devoted to Victorian varieties of mostly annual cut flowers. The citrus plants in their containers are wheeled out onto the terrace for the summer.

Richard Dee introduced *Anemone fulgens* 'de Caen' *(left)* from his home area around Penzance, where it used to be grown as a field crop. This old variety has incredible stamina and our first trial flowered for around six months, right through the winter of 1997/98. Mike Friend *(above)* succeeded in supplying fresh flowers for the Christmas table – and every desk and counter – to cheer those dull days.

What a treat it is to be allowed to pick flowers. ***Rudbeckia fulgida* 'Deamii'** *(above)*, ***Doronicum plantagineum excelsum*** *(right)* and ***Coreopsis* 'Mayfield Giant'** *(far right)* can all be intensively cut. However, over the long season the commitment becomes a time-consuming burden, leaving Mike Friend little time for other summer duties within the Flower Garden, like hedge-clipping.

Accounts dating back to the early eighteenth century record the purchase of rosemary flowers, cherry water, syrup of wood sorrel and conserves of roses by Mrs Mary Tremayne for her young son John, born 1709. By the middle of the eighteenth century herbs were no longer confined to apothecaries' gardens or physic collections. They had become essential requisites for a gentleman's household and would most certainly have been incorporated within plans for the original Flower Garden here. The aromatic and attractively textured foliage and flowers of the herb collection bely their fundamental importance within the productive gardens.

Philip McMillan Browse has re-established a segment in the Flower Garden dedicated to perennial herbs. Against a lavender hedge we grow bergamot, sage,

thyme, rosemary, hyssop, tarragon and winter savoury. Both culinary and medicinal uses are catered for. We also grow a number of herbs annually, alongside the salads and early vegetables. These presently include borage *(right)*, fennel and feverfew *(below)*, several varieties of parsley, summer savoury, chives, chervil and sorrel, dill, caraway and coriander, marjoram and sweet cicely.

In other areas of the garden we have established permanent plots of mint, comfrey, violets, Jerusalem artichokes and garlic.

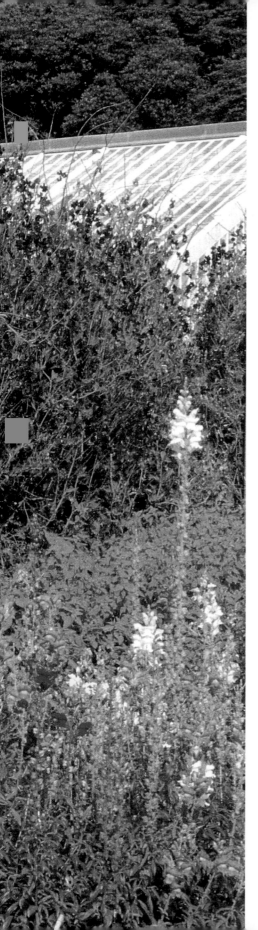

Sweet peas make an English summer: you can dream of nothing better than a healthy, long-lasting show. This requires a great deal of attention, in terms of propping, tying and dead-heading and in the end a shot of rough weather usually seals the fate of our wall of scent. We grow *Grandiflora* 'Mixed' for its variety of colour, including two-tone shades. It is a sad day when the tired crop is rolled up *(above)* and carted away for another year.

Many autumn activities take place indoors. It is particularly important to save the seeds of the rare varieties that we grow, as there is always a chance that we may not be able to obtain them again from outside suppliers. **Richard Dee** *(above left)* **sorts seeds which have been collected from the Flower Garden. We are ever mindful of the danger of cross-fertilization, sowing guaranteed pure strains whenever possible. Simon Lawday** *(above right)* **cleans onions in preparation for stringing and winter storage. Paul Haywood** *(right)* **reaches up to pick a fine bunch of grapes, our first harvest.**

Richard Dee tends his vines *(above)* **– a mirror image of the past? Heather's Vine Man** *(right)* **lost his legs before he ever emerged from his cast; nonetheless the spirit of the old gardeners was returned to the vinery.**

The Melon Garden

This special place is, in both practical and symbolic terms, the heart of the whole garden. From the day John Nelson and I discovered its range of shadowy buildings and skeletal timbers among all that haunting dereliction, it exuded a sense of lost purpose. For us, its restoration was a journey of learning by doing, to find out what had gone on here before. For generations the Melon Garden would have been the hub of all the main productive activities, daily and around the year, supporting the endless cycle of growth and harvest upon which the whole community depended. It was from this place that plant and man set out on their business, and to this haven that they both inevitably returned. Here was the beginning and the end of it all.

The pulse of Heligan has hardly changed over two centuries. The seeds of plants destined for many parts of the gardens would have been sown here in seed trays;

subsequently the seedlings would have been thinned, potted up and brought on in the cold frames. As the weather allowed, healthy plants would have been taken out beyond the safe, curving walls of the Melon Garden to grow and develop over the season, in order to provide flowers and food of incredible range and variety. A succession of pickings would secure a stream of fresh produce from late spring to late autumn. Gathered from both Flower and Vegetable Gardens, everything would be returned to the Melon Garden to be washed and bundled as necessary before being delivered to the back door of the Big House.

The cramped, gloomy buildings of the Melon Garden offered space for all associated activities, including storing and repairing tools and equipment, sorting and keeping fruits and root vegetables for winter, forcing produce for early spring consumption and chitting potatoes for planting the following season. The garden was a place of rich aroma, of manures of various hues and of compost mixes which were kept to hand in bins under the benches of the potting shed. A whiff of damp and the bittersweet tang of creosote and paraffin pervaded everything. Even the early coming of electricity to Mevagissey made little impact here, where weary eyes still smarted from the smoke of the paraffin lamps as dusk descended on winter evenings.

The relentless cycle of the seasons was reflected in traditional tasks common to successive generations of gardeners at Heligan. In addition, the squires of Heligan indulged a passion for cultivating the curious and the exotic under an array of glass. This was the fashion throughout the country and meeting its demands extended the reputation of British gardeners throughout the world. The challenges entailed in restoring the pineapple pit and melon house to function reinforced our admiration for them.

Today, Katharine Cartwright is the foreman of our productive gardens, working under Richard Dee with Paul Haywood, the fruit man, and Mike Friend, the flower man. Charles Fleming and Mike Rundle offer a range of all-round skills and a lifelong commitment of service which makes them central to the productive team. Between them, they set in train all the activities that will lead to a rich harvest, after which everything returns to the snug confines of the Melon Garden, in an endless, unbroken cycle. It was ever thus – almost.

(above left) **A gardener proudly displays a large leaf of *Gunnera manicata*, in front of the pineapple pit with the melon house behind. Does this picture show a character from the team of 1900?**

William Guy, Private Carhart served with the Duke of Cornwall's Light Infantry. Just sixteen months after volunteering he found himself embroiled in the third battle of Ypres – better known as Passchendaele, perhaps the most horrific of First World War battles. He died on 30 October 1917, when the fighting was at its peak. From the history of the regiment, we know: 'The end of October was a veritable nightmare. In the front line conditions were truly terrible. It was bad enough to be shelled and potted at all day and all night ... it was necessary also to be on the alert lest you slipped down the slippery, muddy side of the shellhole into the slime and mud and filthy water at the bottom.' Nobody knows how Percy Carhart died and he has no known grave. He is remembered on the Tyne Cot Memorial to the missing, just outside the village of Passchendaele. His family mourn him still and his niece recounts that his death had further tragic consequences: his sweetheart became inconsolable and died soon afterwards from a broken heart.

Mystery surrounds the fate of Charlie Dyer, who lived on the estate at Heligan Mill. What we know of him is recalled by his grandson, Perren, who still lives in Mevagissey. Charlie was in the Royal Naval Reserve and so would have been among the first to be called up. The family records that at Christmas 1915 Seaman Dyer was serving on board HMS Rosa on Northern Patrol; he was also involved in the Battle of Jutland.

At some point he was wounded and moved to a naval hospital, from which he disappeared. He was registered as a deserter and, at a time when conditions such as post-traumatic stress disorder weren't recognized, his wife and children, one of whom worked at Heligan from the Second World War until the early 1950s, had to suffer all the stigma attached to this.

One thing is certain: some time after his disappearance (it may have been as much as two and a half years) a skeleton was discovered in some woods and a wedding ring identified it as being that of Charlie Dyer. It was presumed he had not deserted and the navy granted his wife the widow's pension she deserved. It didn't heal the pain. Perren remembers that she would always burst into tears at the mention of his name, and wore black until she died in 1966, aged eighty-four. Seaman Charles Dyer's date of death is recorded as 24 May 1918. He was thirty-five. The Commonwealth War Graves Commission still maintains his grave, close to Heligan in the cemetery at Mevagissey.

We shall remember them.

Of R. Barron of Mevagissey, C. E. Ball of Polsue, L. Warne of Trelewack and D. Hocking of St Ewe we have no information other than their names on local memorials, recording that they gave their lives fighting for king and country. We know two more gardeners enlisted: A. Smaldon and J. Varey. What about the others who left their mark in the thunderbox room? The three Paynters, W. Durnsford, Vercoe, Vickery, W. Rose and Albert Rowe. The scent was growing faint when a marvellous letter arrived from Ken Paynter.

Three members of his family had worked at Heligan before and after the First World War: William his grandfather, Richard his uncle and Fred his father. At the outbreak of war William was too old for the army and Dick failed his medical, but Fred served in the 16th Battalion of the Tanks Corps from 1915 to 1919. Kenneth wrote that his grandfather and father were masons and his uncle a carpenter on the Heligan estate. When there was no building or repair work to do at Heligan or on the estate farms they would help in the garden or as general handymen. Kenneth told us about John Claude Tremayne (1869–1949), the last Tremayne to occupy Heligan House:

The last Squire Tremayne had a Rolls-Royce, one of the first in Cornwall. This came complete with a chauffeur who was also a Rolls-Royce-trained mechanic. The wheels had hard rims with spikes, as the roads were in a poor state in those days. When the car reached London Apprentice the chauffeur sounded the 'siren', which was fixed on the front of the Rolls.

Immediately, the Lower Lodge Keeper or his wife had to open the gates; this was so the car could be driven straight in. It always went so fast up the drive that the metal spikes produced sparks on the stones. If Grandpa or other estate workers were working there, they had to stop what they were doing and stand to attention, with their caps off, facing the car as Squire Tremayne went by.

When Squire John died, my father, uncle and myself attended the funeral at St Ewe Church.

(left) **William Guy, aged 14, before he began work at Heligan.**

My father and uncle had the opportunity at the time to go down the Tremayne family vault in the south aisle of the church. Lead coffins were resting on shelves.

Much later, in the 1960s, when Uncle Dick was in his seventies, I took him to Heligan. We walked up through the gardens, right up through the walled gardens to the Bee Boles and the Grotto. It was so overgrown and tumbled down that he became upset; tears filled his eyes so I brought him away quickly. He would have been so proud, as would my father, to see the gardens in all their glory today.

(above) **Only days before this book was to be printed, we came by this early portrait of William Paynter and family. In 1893 his son Fred was a baby. Richard can be seen sitting at his mother's feet. Their expressions convey the trial of sitting still. Ken Paynter gave us copies of newspaper extracts recording William's sixty years service to Heligan before his death in 1943. Could he have been around at the turn of the century? A close look at the first team portrait, at the front of the book, indicates that we are on the trail at last.**

The Heligan Estate Labour Books of 1914–16 *(top)* **offer evidence for the size of the staff and the range of their tasks. We have no need for our team to maintain the many cottages, originally for staff, in and around the estate, but, by and large, they carry out a similar variety of occupations. The record for the week that war broke out, August 1914** *(above).* **March 1915; F. Paynter – left to enlist** *(above right).* **April 1915; R. Paynter – painting peach house** *(right).*

Mar 1915.

NAME	MONDAY. 1	TUESDAY. 2	WEDNESDAY. 3
A. Smaldon	Shop ✓	Shop ✓	Shop ✓
R. Paynter	" ✓	Painting frames	" ✓
J. James	Woods ✓	Fence ✓ Contract	Fence ✓
W. Paynter	Tregarton	Tregarton	Tregarton
F. Paynter	Left to enlist.		
J. Holman	St Austell for lime	Carting sand	Odd Carting
J. Trevenna	" ✓ "	Mixing mortar	" "
W. H. Baker	Woods ✓	" ✓	Mixing mortar
W. King	Tregarton	Woods ✓	" ✓
A. Rundle	Woods ✓	Fence	Fences
O. Gay	Back door repairs		

April 1915

NAME		MONDAY. 19	TUESDAY. 20	WEDNESDAY. 21
A. Smaldon	b	Shop	Shop	Painting Peach Ho
R. Paynter	M	Painting peach house	Painting Carnation House	Par for timber.
J. James	C	Sawing	Sharping saws	Lighting Engine
W. Paynter	M	Trenning drains	Trenning drains	Trenning drains
J. Nicholls	M	"	"	"
J. Holman	L	St Austell for goods & material	½ Carting gravel ½ St Austell for goods John cutting grass +	Par for timber.

Percy Carhart in the uniform of the Duke of Cornwall's Light
Infantry *(above left)*. He died 30 October 1917, aged nineteen.
William Guy in the uniform of the same regiment *(above right)*. He
volunteered in 1914. He died 12/13 April 1918, aged twenty-three.

Charles Ball in the uniform of the Worcestershire Regiment
(above left). **He died 3 April 1918, aged forty-two.**
Seaman Charles Dyer *(above right).* **He died 24 May 1918, aged**
thirty-five.

Old skills relearned. Cutting and bedding 'beaver tail' glass, and positioning the 'lights' on the cold frames *(above)*. The finished article back in action *(right)* — chrysanthemums await planting out.

The restoration of the pineapple pit is Heligan's most significant single achievement. This particular design was undocumented, even at the RHS Linley Library, and it wasn't until two years after its restoration, and hundreds of hours of experimentation, that Richard Dee discovered how to make it work. The manure trenches *(above left)* were excavated in 1992, but it was not until 1996, when Richard joined us, that the secret of manure heating was finally cracked.

Charles Fleming and Simon Lawday wash the manure to make it 'sweet'. Richard layers the manure in the trenches, before sealing it in with weatherboards to retain the heat produced by its fermentation. Simon and Richard lift one of the lights to monitor the progress of the precious pines *(above right)*. In October 1997 Richard was able to display one of his first pineapples, a 'Smooth Cayenne' *(right)*.

This romantic artefact *(left)* represents a crucial part of nineteenth-century husbandry. The collection and use of rainwater was deemed most efficacious. The pot boy would have been on hand. Our superb collection of species fuchsia, all pre-dating 1910, that was recently given to us as a gift, would have been one of the beneficiaries. Presently potted up, many have proved hardy enough to be planted out elsewhere in the garden *(above)*.

Outside the window of the restored potting shed *(left)*, Philip McMillan Browse has established a mint border of many varieties. Some of our large terracotta forcing pots can be seen in the foreground – the tallest for rhubarb and the shouldered ones for forcing seakale and chicory. Inside, Mike Friend uses the potting bench to sort and bundle fresh-cut flowers *(above)*.

Back in 1991 the upstairs window of the two-storey building *(right)* was held in place only by the ivy entwined through its rotting frame. In the original dark house downstairs, restored a few years later, **Katharine Cartwright** *(above)* successfully utilizes the dark, warm space as a mushroom house. Her first crop was so prolific that we were able to supply all the local hostelries.

The brooding presence of the two-storey building *(left)* had drawn John Nelson and I from the first moment we entered the Melon Garden. It was here, in a tiny room inside the right-hand doorway, that we were to come upon the writing on the wall. By 1994, the two-storey building was structurally restored *(below)*. The climbing rose 'American Pillar' *(left)* traditionally screened the working buildings from passers-by.

The return of harvest to the dry, secure confines of the Melon Garden symbolizes, more than anything else, the restoration of the seasonal pulse of the gardens. Barrows full of 'Hollow Crown' parsnips *(far left)* and mounds of 'Detroit' beetroot *(above)* represent but a few of the rich variety of winter roots gathered and stored here every autumn. John Nelson *(left)* has always had a special affinity with this place, coming to get a whisper from the past when the muse fails him.

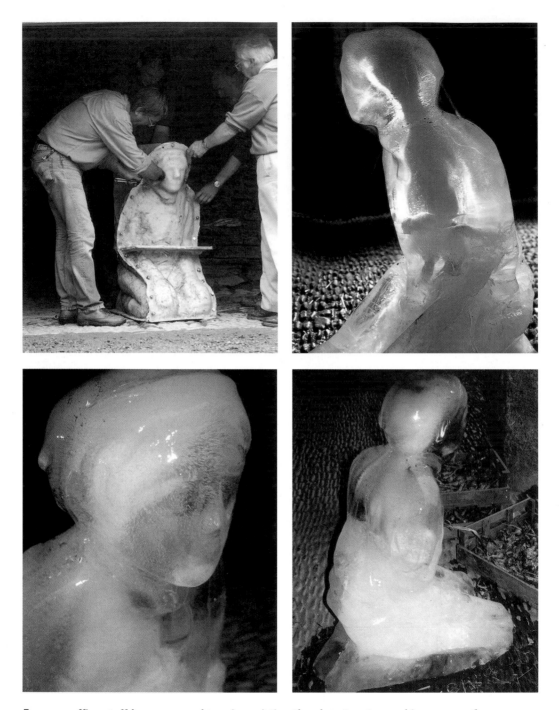

Even our office staff became caught up in assisting the almost metamorphic process of emergence from Heather's casts *(top left)*. **Kneeling Boy, returned to the heart of the garden from the cold, had a simple, haunting quality, bearing an expression of infinite sadness.**

The Vegetable Garden

One of the more specific records that we have come across, so far, of gardening activity at Heligan is for Diggory Abbott. He had worked at Pencarrow and came to Heligan in 1904 with excellent references. In December 1912 he applied for a head gardener's job elsewhere – and what we know of his work at Heligan comes from this reference written for him by the head gardener of the time (reproduced by kind permission of Mr Aubrey Lane, who married into Abbott's family).

What is so remarkable about the letter is that it could have been written today. No matter what the advances in technology, the tasks of a gardener remain broadly the same and the intensive labour associated with previous generations is related to a care and attention to detail that is as crucial today as it ever was. We have experimented with a wide range of traditional tools and found that some modern inventions have advantages – but that by and large these are in peripheral areas. For instance, a chainsaw is quicker than a traditional double-handed cross-cut saw for cutting timber or pruning large branches. In the same way, anyone who has mastered the full-sized scythe will tell you

Station: St Austell G.W.R

Telegrams: "Mevagissey"

Telephone: No.7, Mevagissey

The Gardens,

Heligan,

Pentewan R.S.O

Cornwall.

14 Dec. 1912

Dear Sir,

Diggory Abbott was employed principally out of doors here. There was a re-arrangement of the staff when I came and Abbott was kept as leading hand outside, previous to that he did duty under glass as well – He has a good knowledge of peaches-vines, we have not cultivated oranges here, only so far as a few exist during favourable seasons in open air – He has assisted in the pruning of all the general run of fruit trees, training and tying of the same.

We grow good peaches and he assisted in planting young trees, in lifting and root pruning of them, dressing of the borders and thinning shoots and fruit as a lot of this was done in bad weather and I used him for it more than other outside men –

He can grow Melons and also begonias, gloxinias, and the usual run of annual flowering plants and bulbs –

The charge of a small stove also he could manage –

In regard to men he has had charge of two or three men at times and has managed them well in carrying out different work and should be able to do so when he has full charge of them. I cannot say much about decoration as I have not used him for it at all – He made up a wreath or two very fairly but that is all I have seen of his work in that respect. He knows how to keep up a succession of flowers and vegetables, and once he gets a gauge of what you require should be able to do so well.– This is as clear as I can answer your questions respecting him, and anything further I shall be pleased to do if required.

Yours sincerely

R. W. Norman.

(above left) **Heligan House was a convalescent hospital for officers during the Great War. With a reduced staff, the garden provided respite – and food.**

that a modern strimmer is more comfortable and efficient to use. However, when it comes to plant husbandry the old tools still appear to have the edge and the vexed questions of soil management and the methods employed in combating pests and diseases do not come with easy answers.

Our 1.8 acre (0.72 hectare) Vegetable Garden is dug by hand. No engine-driven rotivators, those invaluable assistants of the amenity horticulturist, will plough their furrow here. Richard Dee forbids their use on the grounds that the perfect fluffy tilth they leave behind is a deception: murdered soil, unable to retain moisture or nutrients. Hand-digging allows seaweed and manure to be turned into an organic glue that retains water and air in the soil, enabling roots to grow better and the plants to become bigger

and healthier. Heligan's friable soil is in very good heart after years of hard work and is the foundation on which the productive gardens build their reputation.

Philip's rotational master plan and regime of seed selection still provide the substantial skeleton on which our Vegetable Garden will continue to be developed. His planning is strategic, yet infinitely adaptable. Each new discovery quickens the pulse and curious special treats are offered and gratefully accepted. A gift of some rare huskless oats, once a part of the local staple diet and treasured in a private collection, was bulked up for future cropping. The Sutton broad bean was rumoured soon to become unavailable so Richard hunted down an extra kilo or two just to be on the safe side.

The productive gardens at Heligan are, by and large, husbanded as they would have been during the nineteenth century. The difference is that for reasons of curiosity and conservation we are growing a wider variety of crops than would have been needed, or practical, to meet the requirements of the Big House.

One of Philip's first ambitions was to grow a collection of traditional potato varieties. These he obtained from Scotland, where the finest potatoes are grown. However, Cornwall is wet and mild which leads to a number of very particular problems. The county has a fine tradition for early potatoes but main crops are a recipe for starvation, with blight, a fungus that loves the warm and the wet, affecting them four years out of every five. The old varieties we chose, which may have been resistant eighty years ago, had become weakened. We knew it was a challenge to buck nature by growing early, second-early and main-crop potatoes in the same ground, especially when the main crop would traditionally have been field-grown. In 1994 we began with maybe a dozen potatoes of each variety. These were planted, bulked up and kept for seed for the following year when we managed whole 100ft (30.5m) rows. But in the warm, still environs of the Vegetable Garden something was moving relentlessly. We had been tempting fate and finally, in 1998, the time for reckoning came.

This confronted us with the broader question of whether to maintain an organic regime in the face of such an intractable problem. The traditional protection against blight, which we had been using, was the ubiquitous Victorian favourite Bordeaux mix, a spray that combines lime and copper sulphate. It provided a barrier which, in a wet

(left) **Mike Rundle was the model for Heather's Scythe Man.**

season, would be very quickly washed off. (Furthermore, the lime could dry out the skin, sting the eyes and damage the lungs of those using it injudiciously.) Indelicate use could also burn the leaves of the plants it was intended to protect. Organic approval of the spray has recently been withdrawn by the Soil Association because of the copper residues it leaves. This means organic growers have no means of dealing with blight. In any case, as we have discovered, traditional fungicides including lime are not much use because most of the really bad fungal infections, such as the mildews, affect the actual tissues of plants. Systemic fungicides and insecticides were only developed well after the Second World War. Although they offer effective control we shall need to investigate the implications of their use.

Heligan is organic by preference, but we realize that an exceptional situation may arise where we have to review this policy. Richard cultivates his vegetables at home this way and is not content to produce crops that he would not feel happy eating himself. These days many chemicals are considered safe: they use integrated controls and are applied as minimum dosages rather than blanket spraying. But the health and safety regulations are so strict that Richard wonders whether it isn't preferable simply to lose the odd crop; besides which, a persistent fungicide could damage the rotation, and persistent pesticides could undo the delicate ecological balance that has been built up over the years. So much work has been done to get the soil into good heart that we have to be very careful not to ruin it.

Considering that we don't use chemicals we don't have many losses. However, there are always problems to entertain the long-suffering gardeners. In 1998 chocolate spot, the fungal infection that affects beans, was an unsightly but relatively harmless ague. The cold weather upset pollination in the runner beans. The climbing French beans disobeyed the rules and outperformed the runners despite supposedly requiring higher temperatures. Flowers don't like the wet and the absence of sun depressed most of them, with the exception of the asters. Gypsophila was a total failure everywhere and our antirrhinums disappointed when measured against the previous year's performance. The good news was that our soft-fruit bushes didn't get mildew. The bad news was that the gooseberry sawfly got to their leaves first. As for the carrots …

Richard has encouraged the staff to experiment with our expanding collection of old tools to see whether they still have a currency. The wheeled Planet precision seed drill is a brilliant contraption, its Heath Robinson appearance belying a most effective tool. The teething problems we encountered owed more to our inexperience than any fault in the machine. The first trial with the carrots, in 1998, resulted in gaps that needed filling. This encouraged the carrot-root fly, which finds the smell of disturbed carrot irresistible. However, only the first generation suffered. The next drilling went well and no replanting was necessary. The skills had been mastered. The Planet seed drill is a precision instrument. You have to get the distance wheel and depth set right and then learn to walk in a completely straight line. Used properly, it saves on seed and there is a lot less thinning to do later. Our staff love it as it leads to good spacings and healthier crops and it will be continue to be used to sow turnips, chard, beet, carrots and lettuce.

Next up – the wheeled Planet hoe. This is an incredible machine that hoes between rows of crops using two curved iron rakes mounted between two wheels. We tried adjusting the gaps between our rows to no closer than 8in (20cm) to allow for the set of its blades. The original advertisements for the hoe at the turn of the century boasted that it was thirty times more efficient than a man. Mike Rundle can already achieve a ratio of fifteen to one. An average bed of twenty rows can be done in two hours. The drawback is that you can't get between the plants in the row, so this still has to be done by hand. However, the Planet hoe can create the impression of a tidy garden in no time at all.

Since Katharine Cartwright's arrival we have moved much closer to a Victorian production level; she regularly squeezes a salad crop in if there is the prospect of land lying unnecessarily idle. We always have a demand for fresh produce and the land that is intensively cropped provides the green anchorage for our most priceless commodity: the soil. Our staff share the same traditions as their predecessors. Their respect for the deep rich soil would have found a resonance in Diggory Abbott as he set out on his quest to become a head gardener – a man of substance.

The structure of the Vegetable Garden is determined by the location of the perennial crops. Philip McMillan Browse went to great lengths to establish an asparagus bed, knowing that it would be some years before our first harvest. In the winter of 1993/94 a 100-ft (30.5m) trench was dug to receive the new plants, set in a layer of sea sand *(right)*, before being mounded up with earth .

Charles Fleming *(below)* has since had the annual task of top dressing the mound with seaweed and now has the pleasant responsibility for its harvest. Another perennial crop grown is rhubarb, of which there are fifteen varieties at Heligan such as 'Timperley Early' *(far right)*. It is harvested in the spring having been forced in terracotta pots.

A view from the south of the Vegetable Garden *(left)* shows the arterial cruciform path network dividing the plot into four sections. In the foreground, on the right, straw is scattered between the rows of assorted soft fruit. Behind, the asparagus bed flourishes alongside rows of cardoons and globe artichokes. Annual crops of flowers and beans are visible on the left.

Charles Fleming *(above)* has travelled miles in the course of his double-digging career. Here, in winter mode, he cuts a lonely figure as he prepares the north-easterly plot for the following season's potato crop.

Tom Petherick *(top)* **plants out the flower borders beside the arched walk through the Vegetable Garden. Gillian Cartwright** *(above)* **rakes between the rows. A few months later the bare canvas has become a blaze of colour, attracting the bees from the bee boles over the wall** *(right)*.

Mike Rundle *(above left)* **on his hands and knees, pinching out seedlings to establish regular spacing between the remaining plants, and** *(left)* **hoeing to keep down the weeds.**

Katharine Cartwright *(above)* **harvests the climbing haricot bean 'Lazy Wife', so called because its leaves wither prior to harvest to enable the beans to be easily garnered. This gives a misleading impression of poor husbandry, much to the chagrin of the staff who frequently have to explain this to visitors.**

As autumn approaches crops are pulled
and left to dry on top of the soil including a
harvest of shallots *(far left)*. **The gardeners
clear out the flower borders** *(left)* **and return
as much as possible to compost** *(below)*.

In Philip McMillan Browse's four-year rotation of crops within the Vegetable Garden, the cucurbit family brings up the rear creating a stunning harvest display while utilizing the remaining nutrients in the soil. Pictured here are the 'Custard White' *(right)* and 'Green Bush' *(below right)* varieties of marrow and the 'Gold Nugget' gourd *(below left)*. In the barrow *(far right)* are 'Golden Hubbard', 'Jack-be-Little', 'Jack-o-Lantern', 'Custard White' (patty pan) and 'Mammoth' or 'Hundredweight'. Thereafter Charles Fleming begins again on his cycle of enrichment, incorporating spent manure from the pineapple pit, through double digging.

Untypically, autumn 1998 had a purple theme, with asters *(above)* of the *Sinensis* type lining the central path and a fine harvest of 'Red Drumhead' winter cabbage *(right)* and 'Cheltenham Green Top' beetroot *(above right)* at the end of Katharine Cartwright's *(far right)* first season as Productive Gardens foreman. The first frost reveals the intricate patterning on 'Ormskirk' Savoy Cabbage *(over)*.

When we first came upon the Vegetable Garden the laurel hedge which lined its eastern and western boundaries had deeply encroached onto the productive area. After clearance we found the remains of chicken-wire fencing which suggested to us that poultry had once been kept here.

In the spring of 1998 Richard Dee built a new pen and reintroduced some old breeds in keeping with the period of the garden. These include Rhode Island Red, Silkies, Leghorns, Black Orpington and Indian or Cornish Game. Keeping chickens close to the Vegetable Garden makes sense in that weeds and damaged fruit and vegetables can be fed to the fowls and their manure is an excellent activator for the compost heap.

The cast for Heather's Scythe Man, modelled on Mike Rundle, had a surrealistic appeal in its own right, even before nightfall. Later, having shed his ungainly armour, he stood at the end of a tunnel of shadows *(below)* drawing the moonlight into himself, reflecting on the ghosts of gardeners past.

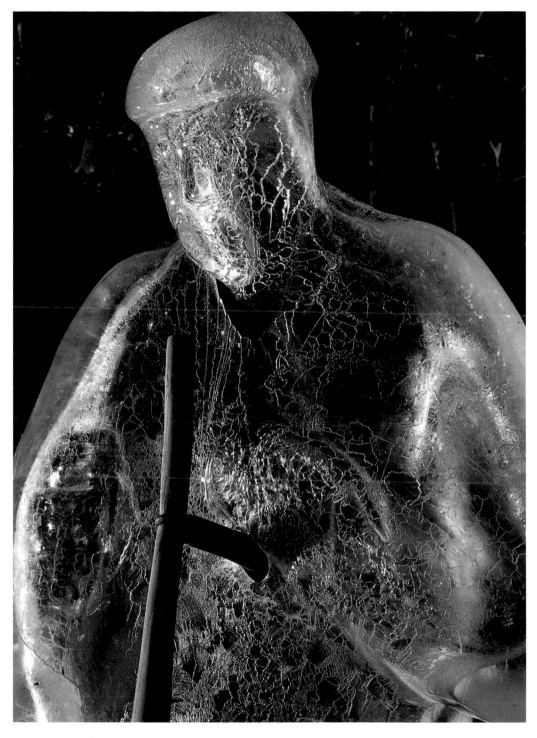

Farewell to the Scythe Man.

Meanwhile **Heather's Hoe Man** *(far right and right)* **cast a shadow over familiar haunts** *(above)* **as he faced his destiny under a mackerel sky. In the morning all that remained were ...**

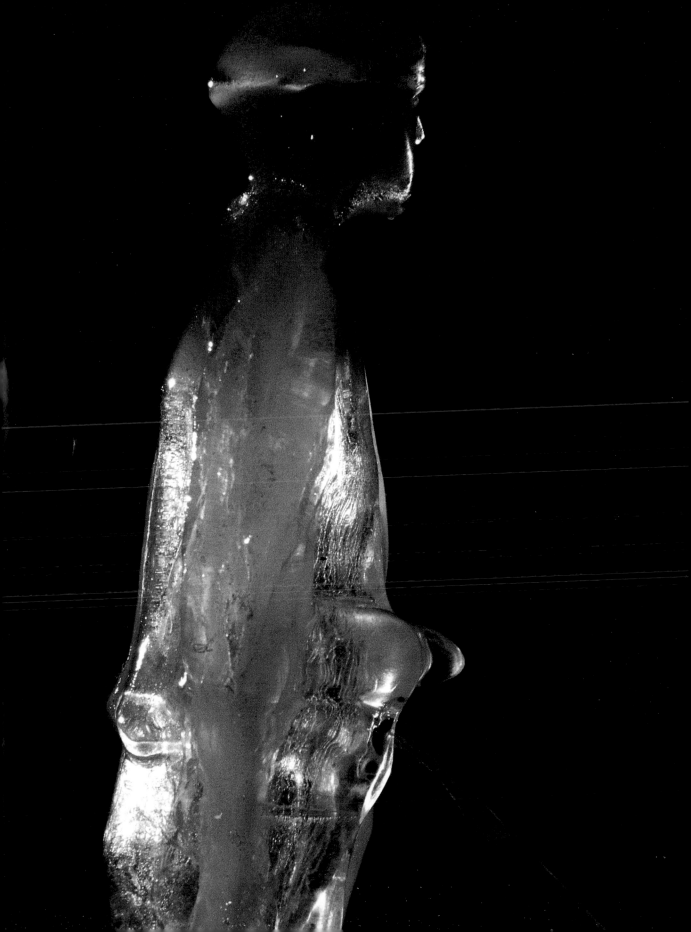

... the memories.

'Yes: of course you can go into the grounds at Heligan. … I am afraid you will find it all rather depressing – as I do, though I hope to get things straightened up a bit presently. – Anyhow; the place will be pleased to see you, … and if you choose a fine day, I hope you will be able to see the ghost of the smile it used to wear.'

Extract from a letter to Mr Ken Paynter written by Sir John Tremayne in 1968, two years before his death which prompted the sale of Heligan House. He had inherited, but never lived at, Heligan.

Index

Acknowledgements

I shall have to record somewhere that Heather's sixth ice mould, Gunnera Man, shot his bolts when he exploded in the Mevagissey cold store, twenty-four hours before the exhibition. What might have been...? I salute Heather for her superb achievement in the face of adversity and we are all grateful to Dartington College of Arts for their support of this project. That the exhibition of ice sculptures took place at all is down to a minor miracle, my new and excellent P.A., Carolyn Trevivan. This was her baptism by fire. I would also like to thank Heather's fellow students and my friend Angus Hudson, for grace under pressure as the experiments took their toll. Sue Hill, her brother Pete and Bill Mitchell deserve honourable mention for being such steadfast citizens on the night in question, working alongside our own magnificent staff who were all out in force to make sure the event happened in the usual Heligan style.

The photographs taken on the night add an extra artistic dimension, as the only enduring record of an event whose transience reflected the passing of an age. I have the greatest admiration for photographers Bob Berry, Charles Francis and Hugh Palmer who understood their responsibilities and went to the greatest of lengths to ensure such fine results.

Above all I would like to extend my appreciation for the generosity shown by the surviving relatives of those who worked at Heligan before the Great War. Their willingness to share their memories – and their bittersweet reflections – has enabled us to pay a more substantial tribute to the people who made Heligan one of the truly great gardens the first time round.

I cannot end without thanking two very important people. Firstly, John Usmar, a local historian and 'Friend of Heligan', whose unstinting research on the gardens, house and wider estate has built such a convincing and intimate picture of Heligan life at the turn of the century. Secondly, Stuart Fraser, a journalist whose tireless enthusiasm tracked down the surviving relatives of staff who used to work here. His sensitivity and tact are a credit to his profession.

Picture Credits

While every effort has been made to provide accurate photographic credits, the publisher apologises for any omissions.

(b) = bottom, (bl) = bottom left, (br) = bottom right, (c) = centre, (cl) = centre left, (cr) = centre right, (l) = left, (r) = right, (t) = top, (tl) = top left, (tr) = top right.

Tab Anstice: 88. Bob Berry with Liz Nolan and Wayne Johns: 2, 44, 45, 46(l), 46(tr), 46(cr), 46(br), 118(bl), 118(br), 146, 147(tl), 147(tr), 149. Channel 4: 29, 65. Lilian Currah/Media South West: 102(l). Sylvia Davies: 10. Perren Dyer/Media South West: 103(r). Charles Francis: 20(b), 21, 24(t), 24(b), 25, 26, 28(bl), 28(br), 30, 32, 33, 34(b), 38, 39, 40, 41(l), 41(r), 62, 68/69, 69, 70/71, 75, 80, 81, 82(l), 82(r), 83, 84, 85, 106(tr), 106(cr), 107, 111, 112, 124, 131, 134(t), 135, 137(t), 140, 141(br), 144/145, 147(b), 148, 150(t), 150(b), 151, 152/153, 154. Philip Guy/Media South West: 98, 102(r). David Hastilow: 13, 14/15, 19, 20(tr), 27, 42/43, 48/49, 58/59, 64, 66, 76(t), 94/95, 104(t), 104(c), 104(b), 106(l), 106(br), 116, 128(t), 128(b), 129, 139, 142/143. Andrea Jones: 8/9, 22/23, 31, 67, 72/73, 78/79, 105, 110, 130. Herbie Knott: 52/53, 113, 114. North Devon Record Office C.R.O. No. B170 add/93/1 (photographed by Charles Francis): 100(t), 100(b), 101(t), 101(b). Marie O'Hara: 86/87. Barbara Palmer/Media South West: 103(l). Ken Paynter: 99. Hugh Palmer: 47, 90, 119, 133, 136. Dawn Runnals: 35, 36, 37, 97, 108, 109, 118(tl), 118(tr). Candy Smit: 115(b). Laura Smit: 6. Sarah Stokes: 122. Claire Travers: 18, 20(tl), 34(t), 74, 76(b), 77, 79, 115(t), 117(t), 120/121, 132(t), 132(b), 134(b), 137(b), 138(t), 138(bl), 138(br), 141(t), 141(bl), 160. Damaris Tremayne: 16, 50, 56.

Peace.